George Washington

by Karen Davila

Boston, Massachusetts
Chandler, Arizona
Glenview, Illinois
Upper Saddle River, New Jersey

Photographs
Every effort has been made to secure permission and provide appropriate credit for photographic material. The publisher deeply regrets any omission and pledges to correct errors called to its attention in subsequent editions.

Unless otherwise acknowledged, all photographs are the property of Pearson Education, Inc.

Photo locators denoted as follows: Top (T), Center (C), Bottom (B), Left (L), Right (R), Background (Bkgd)

All Photos: Library of Congress.

ISBN-13: 978-0-328-67556-2
ISBN-10: 0-328-67556-3

6 7 8 V0FL 16 15 14 13

Who was George Washington?

Washington was a great **leader**.

People chose him to lead.

He was a strong leader.

He helped start our **country**.

He was our first **president**.

Glossary

country a place with the same leaders and laws

leader someone who shows the way for others

president the leader of our country